D1477286

GLOUCESTERSHIRE
from the Air

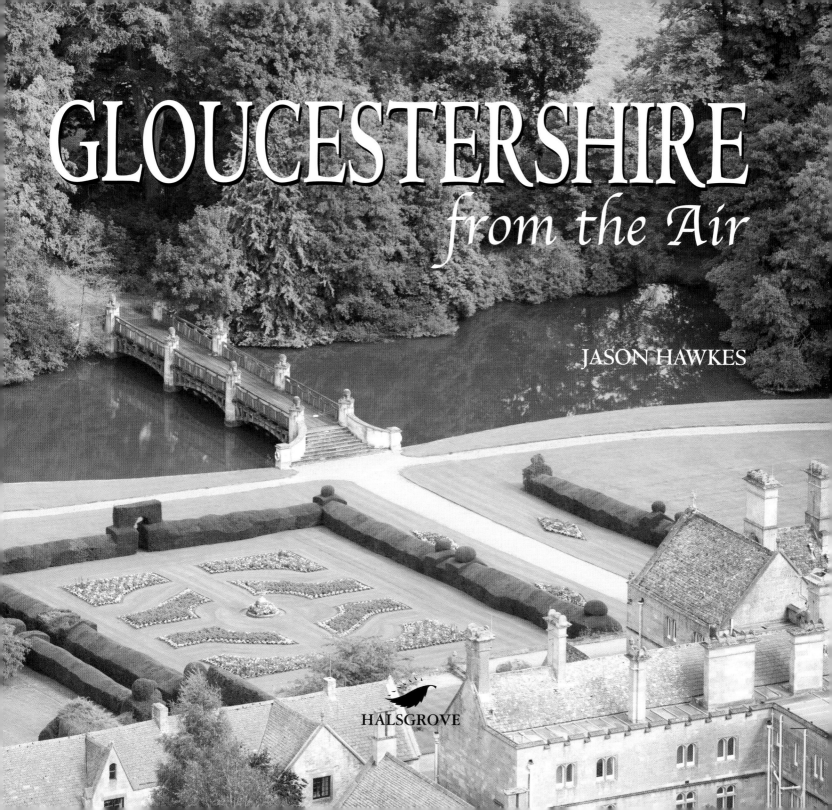

GLOUCESTERSHIRE
from the Air

JASON HAWKES

HALSGROVE

First published in Great Britain in 2010

British Library Cataloguing-in-Publication Data
A CIP record for this title is available from the British Library

ISBN 978 0 85704 002 2

HALSGROVE

Halsgrove House,
Ryelands Industrial Estate,
Bagley Road, Wellington, Somerset TA21 9PZ
Tel: 01823 653777   Fax: 01823 216796
email: sales@halsgrove.com

Part of the Halsgrove group of companies
Information on all Halsgrove titles is available at: www.halsgrove.com

Printed and bound by Grafiche Flaminia, Italy

INTRODUCTION

*H*istoric Gloucestershire is often regarded as the epitome of the English countryside. Covering 3150 square kilometers, the county includes the greater part of the Cotswold Hills, a significant stretch of the broad Severn Valley and the Forest of Dean. Its towns and villages were by and large not heavily industrialized in the modern sense – although the Forest of Dean was notable for its coal mines until quite recent times – but the county has played a key role through the centuries in the growing of wool and the manufacture of cloth. Money from these sources helped to fund the building of many attractive and now mellow country houses and some of the most spectacular churches in England. Towering above them all, of course, being the great cathedral at Gloucester and the abbey at Tewkesbury.

Gloucestershire was always an attractive place for the up-and-coming to settle, partly because of its proximity to mercantile Bristol and partly because of the nearness of fashionable Bath. From the late eighteenth century Gloucestershire developed its own rival to Bath with the growth of Cheltenham Spa, its terraces and houses being some of the best examples of Regency architecture anywhere in Britain. Today Cheltenham is also renowned both for its racecourse and the brooding presence of GCHQ.

But Gloucestershire was and remains a predominantly pastoral scene. Celebrated in music by Vaughan Williams, Holst and Howells, who were all born here, and in words by Laurie Lee, Winifred Foley and Edward Thomas, the county has one of the strongest traditions of living landscape, its hills and valleys, woods and rivers, market towns and gentle villages, being what so many think of as the true soul of England. The fascinating aerial photographs in this book by internationally-renowned photographer Jason Hawkes are selected to provide the reader with an overview of this classic variety of landscapes and settlements, with historic sites included.

The principal attraction of aerial photographs is that they are literally a bird's-eye view, allowing us to look down on the landscape from a perspective that we never normally see. Such pictures reveal to us things that are normally hidden from view, and often surprise us when we find that what we had imagined the layout of the land to be is in reality quite different. The best practitioners of this genre of photography also strive to capture an aesthetic in the images they take, and these pictures, sometimes quite abstract in appearance, are often strikingly beautiful in their own right.

Berkeley Castle. Ancestral home of the Berkeley family, whose ancestor Robert Fitzharding completed the keep around 1189. After the Tower of London and Windsor Castle, it is the oldest, continuously occupied castle in England

Berkeley Castle. Edward II was famously imprisoned and murdered here in 1327.

The Forest of Dean.

Above: Cannop Ponds in the Forest of Dean, were created to supply water to an ironworks at Parkend, highlighting the long traditions of iron-working in the Forest.

Left: Historically, the Forest was the second largest Crown Forest in England, and although properly its borders lie within just five civil parishes, loosely speaking "Forest of Dean" is used to describe all that part of Gloucestershire between the Wye and the Severn.

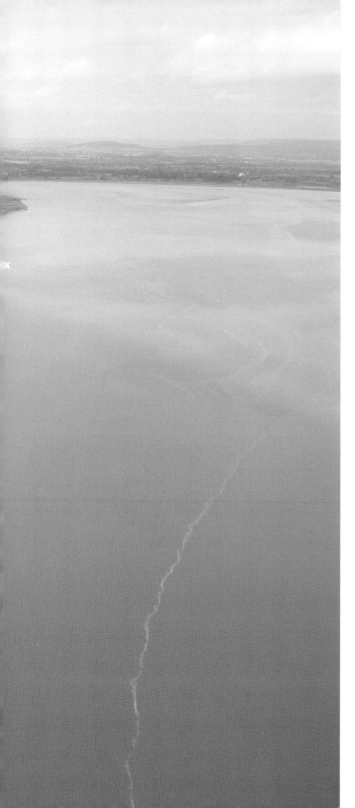

Above: The opposite bank of the River Severn, at Slimbridge. Slimbridge is perhaps most famous for the Wildfowl and Wetlands Trust founded by Sir Peter Scott.

Left: The River Severn at Awre, in the Forest of Dean District. Awre once boasted an important harbour but it is today very much a working farming community.

Overleaf: Rolling countryside at Uley Long Barrow. The barrow is a Neolithic burial mound, known locally as "Hetty Pegler's Trump" after the wife of the seventeenth-century landowner.

Fire Service College, Moreton-in-Marsh. The college is responsible for giving management, leadership and advanced operational training courses for senior fire officers from both UK and foreign fire authorities.

Lechlade is the highest town to which the River Thames is navigable, although the town is actually named after the River Leach which joins the Thames here. The fifteenth-century church of St Lawrence can be seen on the left.

Above: Waterside housing development at Warren's Cross, at the Cotswold Water Park.

Right: The Cotswold Water Park is the largest in the United Kingdom and consists of 147 lakes formed from flooded gravel quarries.

Circular reed beds at Cotswold Water Park. The park hosts a variety of water sports and is popular for birdwatching, although only a few of the lakes are available for public use.

RAF Fairford. Constructed in 1944, after the War it became one of the most significant US Air Force bases in Western Europe. In 2009 it was announced that the USAF would withdraw from the base, after which it would become a "standby base". RAF Fairford hosts the Royal International Air Tattoo, the world's largest military air show.

Above: The present parish church of St Mary, Fairford, was funded by wool merchants John and Edward Tame and consecrated in 1497. It contains the most complete set of medieval stained glass windows in Britain.

Left: Fairford, a small market town on the River Coln in the south east of the county. It was granted its Market Charter in 1135 by Henry I.

All Saints' church, and Down Ampney House, Down Ampney. Perhaps Down Ampney's greatest claim to fame is that in 1872 it was the birthplace of the composer Ralph Vaughan Williams, whose father was the vicar here.

New housing on old gravel pit lakes, South Cerney, in the heart of the Cotswold Water Park.

Above: Quenington, a characteristic Cotswold village, about 8 miles east of Cirencester. According to the 2001 census it had a population of 566.

Opposite: Hatherop Castle. Although the house retains a Jacobean front, it was subject to much mid-nineteenth-century rebuilding under the architect Henry Clutton. It is now a private preparatory school.

Northleach, a town made wealthy by the wool trade of the fifteenth century. The church of St Peter and St Paul, much beautified by benefactions from wool merchants, is known as the "Cathedral of the Cotswolds".

Above: St Lawrence's church Bourton-on-the-Water. The Norman church on Saxon foundations was demolished and rebuilt in 1784. It was reconstructed again in the nineteenth century, but leaving the extremely attractive domed Georgian tower.

Right: Bourton-on-the-Water.

Above: River Windrush at Bourton-on-the-Water.

Left: Bourton-on-the-Water. Bourton, is sometimes known as the "Venice of the Cotswolds" because of the way its low bridges span the shallow river.

Wyck Rissington. Gustav Holst was the resident organist at St Laurence's church here from 1892-3, his first professional engagement.

Market Square, Stow-on-the-Wold. The town was founded by the Abbey of Evesham in the mid eleventh century, as a market place to take advantage of the trade arising from converging roads.

Above: Market Square, and St Edward's church, Stow-on-the-Wold.

Right: In the centre of the square is the Victorian St Edward's Hall, dating from 1878.

Donnington Brewery, established in 1865, near Stow-on-the-Wold. The brewery owns 15 tied pubs around the Cotswolds, and a path called the Donnington Way connects them all.

St David's church at the heart of Moreton-in-Marsh. The church was largely rebuilt in 1858 and the tower was replaced in 1860.

Above: Moreton-in-Marsh railway station lies on the Cotswold Line that links Oxford to Hereford.

Left: Moreton-in-Marsh. The Redesdale Market Hall, in the top centre of the picture, was built in 1887 to the designs of the architect Sir Ernest George. The hall was named for Lord Redesdale, who lived at nearby Batsford Park.

Left: Market day in the High Street, Moreton-in-Marsh.

Above: Farm and outbuildings on the Sezincote estate, near Moreton-in-Marsh.

Sezincote House. The house was remodelled from 1805 by the architect Samuel Pepys Cockerell for his brother, Sir Charles Cockerell, who had made a fortune in the East India Company. The house is a Georgian interpretation of Mughal forms: it is said that the stone was stained to give it an appropriately Indian colouring.

Above: The Cotswold Falconry Centre, situated in Batsford Park.

Left: Bourton-on-the-Hill, with its originally Norman parish church of St Laurence. The main street lies on a steep hill, along which the village developed in the sixteenth century.

Above: Batsford, the parish church of St Mary, a pretty Neo-Norman building of 1861-2.

Overleaf: Chipping Campden.

Opposite: Batsford Park house. The house, built from 1888-92 by architects Sir Ernest George and Peto, sits in the arboretum developed from 1886 by Algernon Bertram Freeman-Mitford (later 1st Lord Redesdale). This was the childhood home of the famous Mitford sisters. The house was sold in 1919 to Gilbert Alan Hamilton Wills, later the 1st Lord Dulverton and in 1984 Batsford Park was donated to a charitable trust founded by the 2nd Lord Dulverton to ensure the future of the arboretum.

Above: Chipping Campden's parish church of St James, endowed by rich wool merchants, was transformed in the fifteenth century into a Perpendicular masterpiece.

Left: Chipping Campden. One of the wealthiest wool trading centres in the West of England in the Middle Ages, its High Street – seen here curving up the middle of the picture – dates from the fourteenth to the seventeenth centuries.

Stanton, called by Pevsner the most architecturally distinguished of the smaller North Cotswold villages. Even the council houses were built in traditional style with local materials.

Stanway Viaduct on the heritage Gloucestershire Warwickshire Railway. Lying to the north of Toddington Station, it consists of fifteen arches and is 210 yards long.

Toddington Manor, bought by Damian Hirst in 2005 and currently under restoration (encased in allegedly the world's biggest span of scaffolding). The house was built between 1819 and 1840 and is notable as a design forerunner of the Houses of Parliament.

The former gatehouse to Toddington House, Church Lane, Toddington. A Jacobean ruin, a remnant of the old manor house, of which the ruined fragments remain 300m south west of the current Toddington Manor.

Central Vehicle Depot of the RAOC (Royal Army Ordnance Corps) at Ashchurch, east of Tewkesbury. It is the MOD's primary distribution and storage site for vehicles, as well as construction machinery, boats and Royal Engineer bridges.

Tewkesbury Marina. The marina sits at the junction of the Rivers Severn and Avon and has 400 flood-protected berths.

Above: The cast-iron Mythe Bridge carries the A438 road across the River Severn at Tewkesbury. 170 feet long and 24 feet wide, it was completed to Thomas Telford's designs in April 1826. Telford proposed a single span so as to reduce interference with navigation of the river, and also to eliminate the expense of constructing foundations in the river gravels.

Left: The historic centre of Tewkesbury, with many medieval and Tudor buildings, including the half-timbered Black Bear Inn, dating from 1308 and the oldest pub in Gloucestershire, which can be seen on the left middle of the picture.

Above: Upper Lode Lock, River Severn, Tewkesbury. The lock and weir were built in 1858, allowing the simultaneous working through of a tug and its train of barges, which is one explanation of the curious shape of the chamber.

Right: Tewkesbury was a flour-milling town for centuries. The Abbey Mill was anciently part of the monastic site, standing on the Mill Avon channel which the monks of Tewkesbury Abbey had constructed. The present mill was built in 1793 and has been converted to residential use.

Tewkesbury Abbey, a Benedictine house, founded in 1092 and consecrated in 1121. The abbey church was saved from destruction at the Dissolution of the Monasteries by the townspeople who bought it as their parish church for £453.

The River Avon, looking from Tewkesbury up towards Twyning.

The Tracy family acquired the manor of Stanway in the sixteenth century and built the romantic house in Elizabethan and Stuart times, not finishing their work until around 1640.

The Vanbrughian pyramid in the grounds of Stanway House, was built in 1750 by Robert Tracy to commemorate his father.

Stanway House. The gatehouse, set at right angles to the mansion, is one of the latest examples of its type, erected around 1630, long after the Tudor heyday of this type of building.

Hailes Abbey ruins. The Cistercian abbey was founded in 1246 by Richard, Earl of Cornwall, younger brother of Henry III and himself later King of the Romans. His son brought to Hailes a relic of Christ's blood, and it became a famous destination for pilgrims. After the Dissolution of the Monasteries it became little more than a stone quarry and the only substantial remains are the skeleton of the cloister.

A Standard tank propels its carriages over a bridge on the Gloucestershire Warwickshire Railway.

Winchcombe railway station. The station, on the preserved Gloucestershire Warwickshire railway, is actually in the village of Greet, about one mile north of Winchcombe itself.

Sudeley Castle near Winchcombe. It dates from the tenth century but the bulk of it as it remains today is chiefly Tudor. Having at one time been a property of the Crown and then in aristocratic hands for several centuries it had fallen on hard times and into semi ruin by the early nineteenth century. It was rescued by two brothers, William and John Dent, who were glovers. They bought the property in 1830 and began a comprehensive restoration. Members of their family still own the castle.

St Mary's chapel, Sudeley Castle, is the resting place of Queen Katherine Parr, the sixth wife of King Henry VIII.

Winchcombe with the parish church of St Peter at its heart. The church is one of the less elaborate of the Cotswold wool churches, its relative simplicity perhaps being due to the former presence of a great Benedictine abbey which stood to the north east of St Peter's, and of which there is now no trace above ground.

Opposite: Bridge over the lake, Brockhampton Park, Sevenhampton. This imposing house, a large neo-Tudor mansion of around 1865, has been converted into apartments.

Above: St Andrew's church, Sevenhampton, with the sixteenth-century manor house adjoining.

Cheltenham Cemetery Chapel and Crematorium. Sited on the north-eastern edge of Cheltenham under the lee of the Cotswold escarpment, the majority of burials and cremations in Cheltenham now take place here.

Above and left: Cheltenham Racecourse. Known as the home of National Hunt racing, it hosts the annual Cheltenham Festival in March in which the feature race is the Cheltenham Gold Cup.

Overleaf:

Pittville Park, Cheltenham, was created in the second decade of the nineteenth century by Joseph Pitt as an area of 'walks and rides' for visitors of the Pittville Pump Room, together with many fine and imposing houses as part of the Pittville Estate development, for the rich and famous who came to live in Cheltenham.

Originally laid out by the architect John Forbes who was also the designer of the magnificent Pittville Pump Room situated at the northern end of the park, it now provides 33ha of parkland, including an ornamental lake with elegant bridges dating from 1827 and a boating lake, formerly known as Capper's Fish Pond. It was named after Robert Capper, owner of Marle Hill House, the grounds of which now constitute the western part of the Pittville Park. The park was formally opened to the public on 25 April 1894, a few years after Cheltenham Borough Council had bought the Pittville Estate.

High Street and St Mary's church, Cheltenham. Cheltenham is actually a town with medieval origins. However, little remains of its pre-Spa history other than St Mary's, the only surviving medieval building in Cheltenham and the parish church of the town.

St Gregory's church, Cheltenham. Designed in 1854 by Charles Hansom, it contains many beautiful stained glass windows by John Hardman of Birmingham, and has been extensively restored in recent years.

Above: Christ Church, Cheltenham, of 1838-40. It was once described as "an outstanding fantasy in the style of a Staffordshire china ornament".

Left: Cheltenham Ladies' College and Imperial Gardens. The college was founded in 1854 but moved to this site in 1873, its new buildings introducing a less than harmonious Gothic tone into the Classical centre of the town.

Above: The Government Communications Headquarters (GCHQ), Cheltenham.

Left: Lansdown Cresent and Lansdown Road, Cheltenham. Designed by J.B. Papworth in 1825, for Pearson Thompson whose father had bought the land on what had once been the outskirts of the town at the beginning of the nineteenth century. The Lansdown Estate was essentially the first English garden city.

The dramatically situated St Bartholomew's church, Churchdown, on the edge of Chosen Hill.

View from Upleadon in the north west of the county, across fields and hedgerows.

Newent. Its dog-legged main street, with attractive brick-fronted Georgian houses, lies to the right of St Mary's church.

Blaisdon Hall, Blaisdon, on the edge of the Forest of Dean. Built around 1876 in neo-Jacobean style, it was used as a seminary and school by the Roman Catholic Salesian fathers from 1935 to 1995. Hartpury Agricultural College took the Hall briefly until 1999 when it returned to private ownership.

Above: Westbury Court Garden, Westbury-on-Severn. A rare survival of a Dutch-style formal garden dating from 1696-1705, now in the care of the National Trust.

Right: Looking towards the Severn Estuary from Boxbush across Arlingham and beyond The Noose.

Littledean, one of the ancient villages of the Forest of Dean. There are the remains of a Roman temple in the grounds of Littledean Hall, but the settlement's most noticeable historic building is probably the former Littledean Gaol, built in 1791, which can be seen in the bottom left of the picture.

Coleford, in the west of the Forest of Dean. The clock tower in the middle of the picture was originally attached to an octagonal church built in 1821. However, by 1882 it was considered too small for the town's population and it was demolished, save for the tower, with a new church being built elsewhere.

Above: Whitecliff Furnace, Coleford. The presence of iron ore and readily available coal led to the development of an iron industry in the Whitecliff Valley. However, a combination of unsuitable and expensive coke and difficult ore led to the abandonment of iron making at the site by 1816.

Left: Whitecliff Quarry, near Coleford, closed in 1976. It has subsequently been developed as an Off Road Centre.

Clearwell Castle, a Georgian "Gothick" house of 1740 or earlier, built by Thomas Wyndham.

Lydney Park was built in 1874-6 by C. H. Howell of Guildford. In its grounds are the remains of a significant Roman temple complex and baths, which themselves overlay an Iron-Age hill fort.

Left: Lydney Park Roman Temple. The temple was built in the fourth century and dedicated to Nodens. Nodens was a Celtic divinity and is mentioned in Irish and Welsh mythology. Many of the artifacts found on this site indicate that Nodens had a connection with the sea. Numerous finds have proved that the occupation extended into the fifth century and indicate that it was a wealthy community.

Above: Picturesque decay at Naas near Lydney.

Above: Lock into Sharpness port.

Opposite: Sharpness lies on the River Severn and is one of the most inland ports in Britain.

Overleaf: Lock on the Gloucester and Sharpness Canal which connects the Severn between the two places, avoiding a stretch of the tidal river which is difficult to navigate.

Above and left: Although its origins date back to the early twelfth century, the present Thornbury Castle was begun in 1511 by Edward Stafford, third Duke of Buckingham. However it had only been partially completed when he was executed, and it remained uninhabited for two hundred years. It was only finally restored in 1854, by Anthony Salvin.

Above: The village of Redwick, in the parish of Pilning, with the River Severn flowing to its north.

Opposite: The Second Severn Crossing, opened in 1996, carries the M4 motorway between England and Wales. It marks the limit of the Severn Estuary and the beginning of the River Severn.

Bristol Filton Airport, in Southern Gloucestershire. This historic site, opened in 1915, has the widest and one of the longest runways in the UK, having been extended for the maiden flight of the Bristol Brabazon airliner in 1949 and again in the 1960s for Concorde.

Hillsley, a small village in the south east of the county. St Giles' church dates from 1851 and was designed by an amateur architect, the Rev. Benjamin Perkins. It has no tower, simply a bellcote.

Above and left: Dyrham Park, near Bath. The baroque mansion was built between 1692 and 1704 for William Blathwayt who was Secretary at War to King William III. The west front facing the garden, seen in these photographs, was designed by William Talman, architect of Chatsworth. It passed to the National Trust in 1961.

Previous page, above and right: Dodington Park near Chipping Sodbury. The great neo-Classical house was built between 1798 and 1813 for Christopher Codrington to designs by James Wyatt. The landscape was laid out around 1764 by "Capability" Brown and adjusted in 1793 by John Webb and William Emes. The Codrington family owned the property from the sixteenth century until 1980. It was bought by Sir James Dyson, the inventor and vacuum cleaner magnate, in 2003 for £15 million.

Above: Worcester Lodge, Badminton – designed by William Kent c.1746, it lies 3 miles in a straight line from Badminton House's north entrance.

Right: Badminton House, the seat of the Dukes of Beaufort. They moved here after Raglan Castle was ruined in the Civil War. Several architects have beautified the house, including William Kent and Sir Jeffry Wyatville, to create what is in essence a palace in the Gloucestershire countryside. The house has many sporting connections: the famous Badminton Horse Trials are held here each spring, and the game of Badminton was popularised here.

Opposite: Deer in the park at Badminton House.

Above and overleaf: Westonbirt House. The house is the third mansion on the site and by far the grandest. The Holford family acquired the estate by marriage in 1665 and in due course accumulated great wealth because of their ownership of shares in the New River Company, which supplied drinking water to London. The present house was built from 1863-70 at the height of their Victorian magnificence. The Holfords also owned Dorchester House in London, where the Dorchester Hotel now stands.

Ozleworth church. The Norman church, which is dedicated to St Nicholas of Myra, is known to have been in existence in 1131. It is cruciform with an extremely unusual central tower, and sits within a circular-walled churchyard. It is now looked after by the Churches Conservation Trust.

Tyndale Monument at North Nibley. Built in 1866 and 111 feet high, the tower commemorates William Tyndale who was born in North Nibley in 1484, and translated the New Testament into English.

Above and right: The market town of Dursley. The parish church of St James the Great used to boast a spire but this collapsed in 1699 and the tower was rebuilt without it. The other building of particular note is the pillared Market House, which dates from 1738 and which lies across the road from the church.

Above: A balloon prepares to lift from a field in Cainscross.

Left: The village of Cainscross, on the outskirts of Stroud, looking up to Ebley Mill. Much of the wealth of the area was built on the cloth industry in the nineteenth century and many mill buildings remain in witness of this.

Ebley Mill, Cainscross. From as early as the 1500s, there was a fulling mill and grist mill recorded at Ebley. Stephen Clissold, built a large mill on the south side of the Stroudwater Canal between 1818 and 1820. The mill was leased by John Figgins Marling in the early 1820s, and later bought by Thomas and Samuel Stephens Marling in 1840. In the 1870s, 800 people were employed in the mill and it had become one of the largest woollen cloth mills in Stroud. It is now used as offices for Stroud District Council.

All Saints' church, Selsley. It was built in 1862 from designs by the young G. F. Bodley through the munificence of Sir Samuel Marling, the owner of Ebley Mill. Bodley also designed the mill tower for Bodley.

Above: Kendrick Street, Stroud.

Left: Stroud. An industrial and trading town, famous for its cloth manufacture which still continues though in much reduced form, today it hosts a prominent artistic community.

Gloucester, the county town, is dominated by the soaring mass of the cathedral, ringed by other churches (Oliver Cromwell once remarked that the city had "more churches than godliness"). The cathedral was founded as an abbey in 679, and re-founded as a cathedral by King Henry VIII in 1541. The city was the subject of radical redevelopment in the 1960s and '70s, proposed in the Jellicoe Plan of 1961. Consequently many of the buildings that surround the cathedral precincts are modern and perhaps unsympathetic to the history of a city which can trace its origins back to Roman foundation as Glevum in AD48.

Opposite: Hawkesbury Monument. The 100ft high Somerset Monument at Hawkesbury Upton, was designed by Lewis Vulliamy in 1846 in memory of Lord Edward Somerset, a general at the Battle of Waterloo of 1815 who died in 1842.

Above: St Mary the Virgin's church, Hawkesbury, a mainly Perpendicular church surrounded by clipped yew.

Above and right: Chipping Sodbury, in South Gloucestershire, a market town built along a spacious street. A town of the utmost respectability, it has endured decades of humorous references, including Kenneth Horne's immortal "I was born on the wrong side of the tracks: the Chipping Sodbury side".

Bitton, in the far south of Gloucestershire, bordering Bristol. A large village of more than 9300 inhabitants, containing some fine buildings, including an ancient church of Anglo-Saxon origins on a Roman site.